Octavio Paz

Octavio Paz

A Meditation

Ilan Stavans

the university of arizona press
tucson

The University of Arizona Press
www.uapress.arizona.edu

We respectfully acknowledge the University of Arizona is on the land and
territories of Indigenous peoples. Today, Arizona is home to twenty-two federally
recognized tribes, with Tucson being home to the O'odham and the Yaqui.
Committed to diversity and inclusion, the University strives to build sustainable
relationships with sovereign Native Nations and Indigenous communities
through education offerings, partnerships, and community service.

ISBN-13: 978-0-8165-2090-9 (cloth)
ISBN-13: 978-0-8165-4256-7 (paper)

Library of Congress Cataloging-in-Publication Data
Stavans, Ilan.
Octavio Paz: a meditation/ Ilan Stavans
p. cm.
ISBN 0-8165-2090-9 (doth: alk. paper)
1. Paz, Octavio, 1914—Political and social views.
2. Paz, Octavio, 1914—Knowlcdge-History.
3. Literature and history—Mexico.
4. Mexico—Intellectual life—20th century. I. Title.
PQ7297.P285 Z9635 2001
861'.62—dc21   2001003282

Printed in the United States of America
♾ This paper meets the requirements of ANSI/NISO Z39.48-1992 (Permanence
of Paper).

Seyd melted the days like cups of pearl,
Served high and low, the lord and churl
Loved harebells nodding on a rock,
A cabin hung with curling smoke,
Ring of axe or hum of wheel
Or gleam which use can paint on steel,
And huts and tents; nor loved he less
Stately lords in palaces,
Princely women hard to please,
Fenced by form and ceremony,
Decked by courtly rites and dress
And etiquette of gentilesse.
But when the mate of the snow and wind,
He left each civil scale behind:
Him wood-gods fed with honey wild
And of his memory beguiled.
 In caves and hollow trees he crept
And near the wolf and panther slept.
He stood before the tumbling main
With joy too tense for sober brain;
He shared the life of the element,
The tie of blood and home was rent:
As if in him the welkin walked,
The winds took flesh, the mountains talked
And he the bard, a crystal soul,
Sphered and concentric with the whole.
That each should in his house abide,
Therefore was the world so wide.

—Ralph Waldo Emerson
Society and Solitude

Octavio Paz

There is no sense in pursuing a literary career under the impression that one is operating a bombing-plane, Edmund Wilson once said. The life of the mind does not kill enemies. Instead, it builds bridges between who we are and who we think we should be. The duty of the intellectual is to serve as a compass, a road map.

More than many in the twentieth-century Hispanic world, Octavio Paz (1914–1998), the Mexican poet and intellectual, was committed to that duty. He was the quintessential surveyor, a Dante's Virgil, a Renaissance man. His complete oeuvre—some 150 titles, which he edited himself and which were released simultaneously in Spain and Mexico as *Obras Completas* in more than a dozen hefty volumes—is a blueprint, an atlas to that most turbulent century, its dusk colored by the same rancor that permeated its dawn. Our self-deprecating dreams, the evil that we do, our insatiable search for happiness amid incessant technological improvements, the value we place on the word, written and oral—all were explored by Paz's itinerant pen, reflecting on the universe in New Delhi and Paris, Cambridge and Buenos Aires, Madrid and Ciudad de México. Much like Wilson himself, Paz was a genuine polymath, a rediscoverer, and a believer in reason and dreams and poetic invention as our only salvation.

I met him only twice—in Ciudad de México in the mid-eighties at an event that also included Borges, Günter Grass, and Allen Ginsberg; and in New York in 1990—and I spoke to him by phone shortly before he was awarded the Nobel Prize for literature. Nothing even remotely a friendship existed between us. But since first encountering him on the printed page, I have been a devotee and incessant reader. No sooner was an essay of his published in *Vuelta* or a volume featured in bookstores, than I devoured it without delay.

Paz would surely have preferred to be remembered as a poet, but his prose is a better metronome for our times. I, at least, consider it an apex. I confess to having never much cared for his poetry. Eliot Weinberger's edition, *The Collected Poems of Octavio Paz, 1957–1987,* is outstanding, but it does not spark my interest. I am intrigued by Paz's experimental poetic drive, by his quest to be a poet engaged with the universe. His poems are about sensations—intangible, ethereal—too close to surrealism, a movement that approached poetry as a form of communion and liberated us all from a tyrannical social order but also let loose the demon of spontaneity. And spontaneity might be a trap: it legitimates chaos and crowns the impetus as supreme ruler.

Jason Wilson argues that "poetry for Paz is not a formal, aesthetic exercise, but it is his very being manifesting itself." Paz did perceive poetry as a soliloquy, a synergy beyond words. Lautréamont, an Uruguayan stationed in France who was a precursor of surrealism, suggested that the day would come when all poetry would be spoken, that people would know it by heart and, thus, it would be lived and not written. Paz agreed: for him poetry was an act of transformation—of himself as poet, of the poem's reader, of the world itself. But I am invariably defeated by his invitation to engagement and get lost in his search for communion. His poetry is too loose, too mystical for my taste.

His nonfiction, on the other hand, is sublime. Even those essays in which he elucidates on poetry itself are inspiring. Often deep into the night, when everything else feels banal, I open *The Bow and the Lyre,* his meditation on poetic revelation, and am quickly hypnotized by it. *Sor Juana, or, the Traps of Faith,* his masterful biography of Sor Juana Inés de la Cruz, takes one through colonial Mexico on a hallucinatory journey almost as mystical in its effect as Sor Juana's own *First Dream:* it leaps across spheres of wisdom, twisting and turning in ruminations that are crystalline in delivery and sharp in content. And his study of eroticism, *The Double Flame,* is as thought-provoking as his reflections on the shortcomings of translation. In fact, it would be impossible for me to name my favorite among Paz's books. What seems easy instead is to recognize the vision that unifies them, a vision made of endless communicating vessels. Each time I read him, I am convinced that every human act has a purpose.

His essays gained him acolytes and enemies the world over, turning him invariably into a cause célèbre. His convictions were perpetually clear, even when they were unappealing. He believed in literature not as a business but an act of faith. It never mattered to him how many copies of his books sold, and many sold poorly. *Leaves of Grass,* he enjoyed remembering, was at first utterly ignored by Whitman's contemporaries, to the point that he himself had to write anonymous reviews of it. Paz was never a best-selling author on the scale of Stephen King, but his influence on our culture and his endurance are infinitely wider and more durable. With erudition and stamina he turned his attention to every aspect of life, from jokes to the paintings of Diego Velázquez, from VCRs to Subcomandante Marcos's upheaval in Chiapas. His style was terse, effulgent, never short of enthralling. By the time he had won the Nobel Prize in literature, he was considered a giant. He was equally at ease discussing T. S. Eliot and Buddhism, the Aztec Empire, Japanese haiku, the balkanization of the former USSR, and the tortuous modernity of Latin America. In an era of obnoxious specialists who know more about less, his cosmopolitanism, his capacious eye, made him a rara avis. Indeed, Paz, as Morris Dickstein said about somebody else, "showed that the role of the generalist is not simply to know a little bit about many subjects, but to be passionate and knowledgeable about many different things—in a sense, to be a multi-faceted specialist." Paz ought to be credited, along with Borges, with opening up the Hispanic mind and making it savvier and more discerning. Because of them, Latin America is less provincial, less cryptic, less clumsy, and more modern. He himself once argued that it became a contemporary of the rest of the world only after World War II. It did so thanks in to his enthusiasm and intellectual stamina.

But what is an "intellectual"? From Antonio Gramsci to Theodor Adorno, the term is loaded with ambiguity. Dwight Macdonald, in a series of articles published by the periodical *Politics,* reflected on the responsibility of the intellectual. He wondered to what extent the American people were responsible for Hiroshima and Nagasaki. Noam Chomsky, in response to Macdonald, described intellectuals as an elite capable of speaking truth to power but which, because of its own commodity, seldom assumes that role. In fact, Chomsky portrays intellectuals right and left as "manufacturers of consent," indoctrinating society in order to alleviate the excesses of its political figures. "The device of feigned dissent, incorporating the doctrines of the state religion and eliminating rational critical discussion, is one of [their] most subtle means, though cruder techniques are also widely used and are highly effective in protecting us from seeing what we observe, from knowledge and understanding of the world in which we live."

My own view is not as radical: I also see the intellectual as an enlightened mind capable of exploring the nature and place of ideas. But unlike Chomsky, I do not believe intellectuals have a duty to any power other than themselves. To survey the territory, the intellectual must take risks, wander about and around with eyes wide open, venture into unforeseen lands, make connections, make use of any tools at his disposal, and not take anything for granted in order to seize the meaning of his environment in full scope.

Full scope. Paz's odyssey is a map to the artistic ups and downs of the twentieth century. He never vacillated in his scrutiny of the ideological trends that came before him (Marxism, communism, surrealism, utopianism, liberalism, etc.). He was an adventurer who might have grown inflexible and exasperated by the modes of his age, but he never ceased to articulate his thoughts on them—to make a map of the currents and countercurrents that shaped him and his environment. It was not always easy to empathize with him. The self-congratulatory trait of his personality became more evident in his old age, and so did his stubbornness. Still, it is impossible not to admire his scope.

This essay is not by any stretch an introduction to Paz, although I hope it brings the uninitiated to his work the way his essays on the Marquis de Sade led me to Justine, and *The Labyrinth of Solitude* (a book I have read so many times I have almost memorized it) attracted me to the works of José Vasconcelos and Samuel Ramos. My objective is to trace the roots of Paz's thought using a biographical template, to place him in context—to make his odyssey meaningful. More than anything else, I want to understand his legacy by explaining its pros and cons to myself.

P az was born into a typical middle-class Catholic household, just as the peasant revolution of Emiliano Zapata and Pancho Villa was getting under way. Modernism was bubbling in Europe at the time, and so was *modernismo* in Spanish poetry—a romantic literary movement that started in 1885 and included authors such as Rubén Darío and Julián del Casal. A few years earlier, Marcel Duchamp, about whom Paz would write a slim theoretical volume in 1968, shocked the world with *Nude Descending a Staircase.* (In Spanish Paz's book is part of volume 6 of *Obras Completas;* in English the essay is titled *Marcel Duchamp: Or the Castle of Purity* and was released in 1970.) Igor Stravinsky had just finished *The Rite of Spring,* and D. W. Griffith was about to release *The Birth of a Nation.* When he was only a few months old, his father joined Zapata's forces while his mother took refuge, with him, in Mixcoac, in the house of his paternal grandfather. Decades later, Paz would describe Zapata's project as an attempt to return to origins. The paradox of *Zapatismo,* he would argue, "was that it was a profoundly traditionalist movement; and precisely in that traditionalism its revolutionary might resides." Later on, as a poet, he turned Zapata into an inspiration.

With the exception of a few years in the United States, where his father, a lawyer and journalist, sought political asylum, Paz spent much of his childhood and adolescence in that house in Mixcoac. When he was a schoolboy it was obligatory to attend mass, but Paz's temperament was not a religious one. For more than three decades, Mexico had lived under the dictatorship of Porfirio Díaz, considered until very recently a tyrant who nonetheless brought prosperity and foreign investment into the nation and helped transform it from a rural landscape to a vibrant republic by building a complex railroad network. The woman Paz's father married was a pious, uncultivated Catholic, affectionate and supportive, who was descended from Spanish immigrants. The child would come to describe his mother as "a love letter with grammatical errors." Later his father became an alcoholic and died in a train crash in 1935. The family owned a substantial library. It was a place where the future poet found escape and early solace, a place that for a while he perceived as a map of the universe.

The adolescent Paz was a passionate student who would fervently discuss politics in the streets, loved Dostoyevski, and joined a student strike in 1929. French culture, too, was essential in his upbringing. During the late nineteenth century, Parisian culture, glamorous and romantic, was glorified from the Rio Grande to the Argentine pampas. The *modernistas* emulated the decadent romanticism of J. K. Huysmans. Latin American poets and painters imitated the rhyme and taste of art nouveau, while the bourgeois saw the tongue of Victor Hugo and Flaubert as a sign of sophistication. This transatlantic influence left an indelible mark on Paz. As a young man, he dreamed of a visit to Paris, and he would eventually live there for three years (from 1959 to 1962) and become a devotee of Baudelaire and Rimbaud.

Were the Americas ever authentic? This is a difficult question. I have tried to tackle it from a personal standpoint in my memoir, *On Borrowed Words*. The *Oxford English Dictionary*, never bashful in its definitions, depicts *authenticity* as the "quality of being authentic, or entitled to acceptance . . . as being authoritative or duly authorized." But where does authority derive from in a hemisphere that became part of Western civilization in a forceful, haphazard fashion? The pre-Columbian legacy and the incoming European culture interbred. The result was a hybrid mix, an either/or impossible to solve. This explains why the collective soul in the region is always divided.

Throughout his life Paz was overwhelmed by this duality. But he never endorsed nostalgia, not even in his most fervently rebellious student years. On the contrary, he invariably took the side of cosmopolitanism. He viewed the European presence in Mexican culture in particular as a necessary evil. Despite the many attacks on his position, Paz always sought to rehabilitate the image of the conquerors. He saw little point in a one-sided portrayal of Spaniards and other transatlantic newcomers as "abusers." After all, their impact on native culture was ubiquitous, undeniable, and indelible. He did not settle for the easy liberal polarity oppressor/oppressed but attempted to understand the side effects of the historical encounter between the Old World and the New. "The empire that Cortés founded on the remains of the old aboriginal cultures," Paz wrote in *The Labyrinth of Solitude,* "was a subsidiary organism, a satellite of the Spanish sun. The fate of the Indians could have been that of so many peoples who have seen their national culture humiliated but have not seen the new order—the mere tyrannous superimposition—open its doors to the participation of the conquered. The state founded by the Spaniards was an open order, however, and deserves a sustained examination, as do the modes of participation by the conquered in the central activity of the new society, that is, religion."

This nonliberal approach set the tone for criticism: Paz did not idealize the victim and vilify the victimizer. His thesis is more complex. It recalls Jean-Paul Sartre's argument in *Anti-Semite and Jew* that Jews need anti-Semites to exist, and vice versa. Likewise, Paz insinuates that in our eyes black is black because of the memory we have of white and, similarly, white is perceived as a counterpart of black—its other side. In other words, Mexican civilization is not a subtraction but an addition: it is made of the

Spanish *and* aboriginal ingredients.

This dialectic of opposites is typical in Paz: East/West, reason/desire, word/silence. And yet the argument itself is ubiquitous in other thinkers and artists. An example: Joseph Brodsky, the émigré Russian poet and Nobel Prize laureate (once one of Paz's close friends) develops this view in the poem "To Yevgeny," part of *Divertimento Mexicano,* drafted in a trip to Mexico in 1975. The poem strikes me as a summa, albeit an indirect one, of Paz's own interpretation of the nation's character. In 1991 I asked Brodsky about the poem's thesis that Aztecs would never have been able to find out who they were had it not been for the Spaniards. His reply: "It is a reaction to what I saw. It is exactly the same thing that the Russians say about the Tartars or the Mongols: they ruined our historical development. It is a racist attitude that seeks to blame foreigners or invaders for the nation's problems. The Tartars gave Russians cohesive statehood, they unified the country. The same thing with the Mexicans in regard to the Spaniards: they blame them for their past, forgetting that thanks to them they have their language and literature."

In the thirties Mexico's capital was lively but also confining. "Youth is a time of loneliness but also of passionate friendship," Paz once announced. And so he made friends. Through books, Paz's Mixcoac upbringing allowed him
vistas to alternative realities. But toward the nation as a whole he felt disconnected, cut off. As a middle-class adolescent, he asked himself: To what extent am I an integral part of this place and its history? His reply came in the form of a trip. At twenty-two years of age, he felt suffocated. He had enrolled in the Colegio de San Ildefonso, which the government turned into the National Preparatory School. But he was unhappy and decided to drop out of college and also to leave home. "I had a hard time," he later said, "but not for long." The Mexican government had established secondary schools in the provinces for workers' children, and he was offered a teaching job in 1937. The school was in Mérida, in the Yucatán peninsula.

Like a seashell, the word *Yucatán* awoke echoes in my mind that were both physical and mythological: a green sea, a calcareous plain networked with underground currents like the veins of a land, and the vast prestige of the Maya and their culture. More than distant, Yucatán was isolated, a world closed in on itself. There was no train or road; there were only two ways to reach Mérida: a weekly plane or by sea, very slowly, in a boat that left once a month and took two weeks to travel from Veracruz to the port of Progreso. The upper- and middle-class Yucatecans were not separatists, but isolationists: when they glanced abroad they did not see Mexico City but Havana and New Orleans. And the greatest difference: the dominant native element was the Mayan, descendants from the *other* ancient Mexican civilization. The real diversity of our country, hidden by the centralism inherited from the Aztecs and Castilians, was patently obvious in the land of the Maya.

Ironically, just as Paz fell in love with the aboriginal aspects of his country's culture, his literary vision began to be tarnished by surrealism. An unusually precocious writer, he had published his first book of poetry at age nineteen, one he later criticized as inflammatory and too rhetorical. He would not consider himself an essayist until after reaching thirty-three, as he began to shape his masterpiece, *The Labyrinth of Solitude,* the book that made him an instant celebrity. Again, this so-called return to the sources ought not to be seen as an identification of young Paz with the lower classes. In fact, his experience in Yucatán and elsewhere in the southern states of Mexico brought a good deal of physical discomfort and intellectual puzzlement. His individual identity too emerged as divided: Was his *mexicanidad,* his "Mexicanness," a denial of *lo europeo,* the European heritage? Could he balance the two— become a bridge across the ocean where the New and the Old Worlds could communicate?

At about that time Paz married Elena Garro, eventually the author of the classic *Recuerdos del porvenir*—translated into English under the Proustian title *Recollection of Things to Come.* (In 1939 Garro gave birth to their only child, Helena Paz, to whom Paz remained distant throughout his life.) Suddenly, while he was still in Yucatán, a twist of fate allowed him to leave the country. This was fortunate because distance and the experience of a self-imposed exile of sorts allowed him answers to internal questions he might never have arrived at had he remained in Mexico. He received an invitation to take part in the International Congress of Anti-Fascist Writers, held in Valencia and other Spanish cities. Again, history wanted him to witness a fundamental twentieth-century human transformation: the first one, the Mexican Revolution, he was invited to tangentially through his father's itinerant ordeal; he arrived at this second one, the Spanish Civil War, by his own merits as a neophyte poet.

The other invitee from Mexico was Carlos Pellicer, an imagist poet who collected pre-Columbian artifacts. The two sympathized with the Socialist cause, but neither was a member of the Communist Party. Paz went to the Iberian peninsula penniless, in search of adventure— much like young Hemingway, but for rather different reasons: he came less as a man of courage than as a man of ideas, and he sought less to prove and promote his manhood than to acquaint himself with left-wing utopias. There he met the militant poet Pablo Neruda, whose Stalinism he soon found repellent. He also met

Rafael Alberti, Stephen Spender, and Ilya Ehrenburg. Yucatán had opened the door to an introspective journey, but Spain moved him in another direction: an unrestrained quest to place Hispanic civilization in perspective—as an octopus with its tentacles everywhere.

In his essays politics is always a crucial factor. In Spain he was enthusiastic about the Republican cause, but he became disappointed by its weak morality. In his book *Itinerary,* Paz eloquently described his ambiguity toward the cause.

> Those inspiring days in Spain meant to me the apprenticeship in a fraternity faced with death and defeat; the encounter with my Mediterranean roots; the realizing that our enemies are also human beings; the discovery of criticism in moral and political spheres. I discovered that the revolution is a child of criticism and that the absence of criticism has killed the revolution.

Once the congress was over, Paz remained in Europe. The experience proved invaluable, for it allowed him to be submerged in the subversive artistic atmosphere that would eventually change our global perception of reality. In his pilgrimage he was befriended by the Peruvian poet César Vallejo, the filmmaker Luis Buñuel ("whose work," Paz argued, "tends to stimulate the release of something secret and precious, terrible and pure, hidden by our reality"), the poet and dramatist Miguel Hernández, and a number of other artists and writers. And yet his tender age (he was twenty-two) made him something of an outsider.

Many years later, Paz, with his typical grandiloquence and absence of humility, would describe his voyage to Spain as a rite of passage not only for him but also for the Hispanic world as a whole. Looking back, he would criticize Neruda's Marxist dogmatism. He would also embellish, perhaps even falsify, his personal experience in the battlefield. Such a refurbishing of the past was not unusual for him. History, in Paz's eyes, was a grand stage, "a ghostly procession without meaning or end" where he was the leading actor and sole protagonist, every instant of his life enlightening to others. For him, historical knowledge was nonchronological. He often mixed autobiographical insights and factual information, thus becoming his own sole object of worship. Despite his bitterness toward the crossroads between politics and letters, between the pen and the sword, the two have always been his obsession. Paz wrote:

> The history of modern literature, from the German and English romantics to our own days, is the history of a long, unhappy passion for politics. From Coleridge to Mayakowski, Revolution has been the Great Goddess, the eternal beloved, and the great whore to poets and novelists. Politics filled Malraux's head with smoke, poisoned the sleepless nights of César Vallejo, assassinated García Lorca, abandoned Machado in a village in the Pyrenees, locked Pound in an asylum, dishonored Neruda and Aragón, has made Sartre a figure of ridicule, and has acknowledged Breton all too late.

Politics also blinded the Mexican. It was only through politics that he might change the world, but were the theoretical systems available truly effective? Would they be successful if and when applied to the Hispanic Americas? But youth is colored by fervor, and before he had the chance to examine the ideological trees of his time fully, objectively, and from a distance, he needed to taste their fruit, to be at once a witness and a participant in them. To equate Marxism with a higher spirituality was young Paz's primary goal. His concern with man's loneliness in the world (a state he believed could be transcended only through faith, compassion, and sexual love) emerged from his antireligious sentiments, from his courage to rebel and experiment, but also, and more concretely, from his desire to find solutions to social problems. In this respect, André Breton, the French surrealist, was a beau ideal. "In my adolescence," he wrote in his book *Alternating Current* (1967), "during a period of isolation and exaltation, I read by chance some pages which, I learned later, form chapters of *L'amour fou*. In them Breton describes his climb to the summit of the Teides, in Tenerife. That text, read almost at the same time as Blake's *Marriage of Heaven and Hell,* opened the door to modern poetry for me."

However impractical, Paz's ultimate political message in these and other essays is that society will return to its original freedom, and men to their primordial purity. Then History, with a capital *H,* will cease. Are we, he asks, living at the end of time? His answer is staunchly in the affirmative. He thinks that modern time, linear time, the homologue of the ideas of progress and history, ever propelled into the future, is coming to an end: "I believe that we are entering another time, a time that has not revealed its form and about which we can say nothing except that it will be neither a linear nor a cyclical time. Neither history nor myth. The time that's coming, if we really are living a change of times, a general revolt and not a linear revolution, will be neither a future nor a past, but a present."

The sources of this idealistic view were not only Rousseau and Nietzsche but also mysticism and Hindu religion. When he could, he criticized (though in a reverent tone) European rationality for imprisoning man; he considered the dreams of reason to be horrendous. In the tradition of Buddhism and even early Christianity, what was left, he thought, was to search for the inner world, to dream with the eyes closed, to look for the eternal present. It is quite obvi-

ous that, at this point, Paz had moved from
Marxism through anarchy to a view of society
characterized by a form of solipsism. Contemporary problems, he thought, were a result of
man's anomie. The burden of the past was too
oppressive. What was needed was regression, a
search for origins.

Paz took his role as intellectual seriously and
understood the challenge of his age. How
to be simultaneously an outsider and an insider
in the society we happen to be part of? The role
of outsider allows for objectivity and clarity. But
that objectivity and clarity are only of value
because we ourselves are, as insiders, the subject
of our own scrutiny. Paz's experience in Spain in
the thirties pointed to an unavoidable fact: the
Hispanic world is utterly uncritical. Criticism,
he once said, "is the apprenticeship of the
revising imagination—an imagination cured of
fantasy and resolved to confront the world's
reality." He was, at his core, a critic. Even as a
poet he comes across as a reflective, metaphysi-
cal troubadour. This poem from *Days and*

Occasions (1958–1961) is symptomatic:

> In the patio a bird squawks,
> a penny in a money box.
>
> Its feathers are a little air,
> and vanish in a sudden flare.
>
> Perhaps there's no bird, and no man
> that one in the patio where I am.

In fact, he devoted his life to the study of poetry, its currents and undercurrents. These studies eventually resulted in *Children of the Mire: Poetry from Romanticism to the Avant-Garde,* the Charles Eliot Norton Lectures delivered at Harvard University in 1982–1983. In them he investigates the power and presence of poetry in the modern world, its impact and function. His research was expanded in his collection *The Other Voice: Essays on Modern Poetry* (1991), where he focuses on Walt Whitman, Rimbaud, Eliot, and Martí. His claim was that poetry, although elitist and apparently unimportant when it comes to historical and scientific progress, is the only true habitation of the human soul—that one can measure the sensibility of an epoch through its most mature verses even if they are unread by the masses.

From early in his career, Paz nurtured the idea of the poet as a hero of modern times, a visionary with a complex understanding of things earthly (sexual, social, political, scientific) who nevertheless prefers to surround himself with muses. He once said, "Poetry, which yesterday was required to breathe the free air of universal communion, continues to be an exorcism for protecting us from the sorcery of force and of numbers. It has been said that poetry is one of the means by which modern man can say No to all those powers that, not content with disposing of our lives, also want to rule our consciousness. But this negation carries within it a Yes that is greater than itself." Indeed, Paz's magisterial oeuvre is a guided tour through the intellectual debacles of the twentieth century and a representation of the poet as a sort of clock of humankind. In "Nocturne of San Ildefonso," one of his finest poems, he claims, "Poetry, the bridge suspended between history and truth, is not a way toward this or that: it is to see the stillness within movement."

In retrospect Paz's ideological swing, from left to center and eventually to a more conservative position, is a map to the circuitous path of Latin America's twentieth-century intelligentsia. This is not a full-fledged biography but a profile-cum-reflection on an intellectual pilgrimage; hence, I cannot stop in every port of call. It shall suffice for me to say that, on his return to Mexico, Paz remained loyal to his left-wing principles. But a turning point took place when, on 23 August 1939, the German-Soviet pact was signed between Hitler and Stalin. Paz and his friends had been supporters of socialism. This meant a muscular antifascist stand. The embrace between Germany and the USSR deeply dismayed him. A clash arose between what he thought and what he felt: Where should he place his hopes? Was there still a set of values he might embrace?

A watershed experience, outside Mexico again, solidified his intellectual convictions at a time when ideological confusion seemed to be the pattern. He left, first for the United States, then for France and elsewhere. He was awarded

a Guggenheim Fellowship in 1943. He stationed
himself primarily in California and New York.
The Belgian Victor Serge introduced him to the
pleasures of *Partisan Review,* an influential

periodical in which Paz read George Orwell ("an
economy of language, clarity, moral audacity,
and intellectual sobriety: a virile prose") as well
as the cadre of New York Jewish literati. And he
used his time—and money—to focus his
attention on what would be his most outstanding accomplishment, a nonfiction masterpiece
that investigates the Mexican psyche without
taking any hostages: *The Labyrinth of Solitude.*
In it he articulated, in lucid, erudite, nonaca-
demic prose, and with Olympian authority, the
key to the question he nurtured in his heart for
years: What does it mean to be a Mexican in
today's world?

This set of interrelated essays, serialized in
magazines, released in book form in 1950, and
reprinted in an updated edition nine years later
(Paz nurtured a Whitmanesque obsession for
updating his books, not only in order to eradi-
cate typos but also, in a Gargantuan fashion, to
eat up his critics' arguments by including their
comments in the form of appendixes), is a

cornerstone in my own political and cultural awareness. I have discussed it in some detail in *The Hispanic Condition,* but I feel the need to return to it again, albeit briefly. Paz's goal was to explain the nation's inferiority complex, *"el sentimiento de inferioridad del mexicano,"* and what he viewed as its ambiguous relationship with life, love, and death. "I do not claim to do anything but clarify for myself the sense of certain experiences," Paz humbly stated, "and I admit that perhaps its only value is as a personal answer to a personal question." But this humbleness hid the ambitious drive behind the enterprise. He set out to ruminate on folklore, history, politics, cosmology, and psychology.

He himself proposed Alfred Adler, a disciple of Freud, and also Otto Rank, as fountains of inspiration. José Ortega y Gasset's philosophical inquiry was also significant, as were, it seems to me, the essays Borges published in the Buenos Aires monthly *Sur* about the Argentine character. A number of precursors, some immediate and others more remote, also need to be taken into consideration, among them José Vasconcelos, in particular the introduction to *La raza cósmica* (the introductory chapter entitled "*Mestizaje*"), and Samuel Ramos, responsible for *Profile of Man and Culture in Mexico,* a provocative if somewhat stilted meditation on *el peladito,* Mexico's street rascal. (Paz: "Ramos analyzed an isolated type and omitted a historical examination," refusing to see "life as relationships." He never linked "Mexican history or the Mexican's vitality with certain universal ideologies.")

The image in Paz's title, a metaphorical reference to the baroque structure of endless doors and forking paths Hispanics call home, is now frequently invoked when referring to reality south of the Rio Grande. (The labyrinth, by the way, a feature in the art of Borges and Kafka alike, seems to be a bridge linking Eastern Europe to the Americas.) This structure, Paz suggests, is a palace of seclusion, of aloofness and sequestration. Indeed, the concept of *soledad*—not really solitude but aloneness— encapsulates the way in which Mexico has embraced modernity: stoically, with resignation, apart from the rest of the world, like an ostrich.

In eight chapters and an epilogue, Paz develops an argument governed by two insights: the view of his countrymen as reticent, introverted, and alienated from Western civilization; and the view of history as a trauma difficult to overcome. He claims that Mexicans, like W.E.B. Du Bois's Blacks in *The Souls of Black Folks,* have a personality cut into halves, a split conscience that is part Iberian and part aboriginal. When Hernán Cortés, a knight whose ideas of honor and loyalty were grounded in medieval times, and his *conquistadores* took control of Tenochtitlán in 1523–1525, instead of eliminating the native Aztec culture to build on its ruins, they mixed, combined, and syncretized themselves with the environment—that is, they used the existent infrastructure to build a totally different architecture. Then too, instead of battling the Spanish intruders, Moctezuma II and Cuauhtémoc, the last two native emperors, welcomed them with precious gifts. Their unexpected attitude—magically studied by Barbara Tuchman in *The March of Folly*—was based on the certitude that Quetzalcóatl would one day return by sea as a bearded white male. The bloody clash between the colonial dream of conquest and the aboriginal festivity dedicated to the Almighty's second coming, in Paz's view, marks the birth of the dark-skinned race, *el pueblo mestizo,* that populates Mexico. Hence, Columbus and his beneficiaries might be seen as incubators of a new people. Add to this history the cautionary tale of Cortés's mistress and interpreter, "La Malinche," whom the conquistador abused and used to communicate with his enemies. He also impregnated her and left her without acknowledging his descendants. From this tale, which I examined in some detail in my essay "Translation and Identity," a clear picture emerges of the male and female archetypes, *el hombre abusivo* and *la mujer abierta,* the macho and the prostitute, that preside over Mexico's conflicted self.

A couple of leitmotifs are the mask and the pyramid. Paz uses the former to explain the facades behind which Mexicans hide themselves; the latter he invokes to analyze the hierarchical structure of the nation's society. Much ink has been devoted to elucidate the message of this book, so I shall not enter into more detail on these matters. But one aspect that intrigues me profoundly does not seem to have generated much interest. It is among the work's most enigmatic elements and it announces the position Paz himself takes vis-à-vis his topic: the elusive "I" he fashions, at once an insider's and an outsider's voice. On occasion the "I" becomes *un nosotros,* a "we," but the outcome in general remains the same: partial restraint. I quote: "The Mexican, whether young or old, *criollo* or *mestizo,* general or laborer or lawyer, seems to me to be a person who shuts himself away to protect himself: his face is a mask and so is his smile. In his harsh solitude, which is both barbed and courteous, everything serves him as a defense: silence and words, politeness and disdain, irony and resignation."

The device is puzzling. Is Paz himself the object of his study or is he not? Does he too suffer from an inferiority complex? Where does he find the authority—that is, the authenticity—to speak about Mexico as if *sub specie aeternitatis?* Mine is not a critique in the destructive sense of the term, though. Had he not found an "in-between" voice, *The Labyrinth of Solitude* might have been ineffectual. What makes it a tantalizing performance is not only the knowledge that Paz instills but also the pseudo-objectivity he persuades us he has found. The reader perceives him as an anthropologist of sorts. But he is not; he is simply a spectator, and a rather subjective one: a Mexican drafting a study of his people, and tangentially of himself as well, from afar—from the other side of the border. This makes the work at once biography and autobiography, in my eyes a most delicious mix. For in the end, isn't biography as much about the observer as it is about the observed? (Perhaps the only chapter in which this in-betweenness does not succeed is also its first and most controversial: "The *Pachuco* and Other Extremes.")

"Mexican history," Paz once announced, "can be seen as a search for ourselves, deformed or masked by foreign institutions and of a form that expresses us." History and politics—the crossroads where these two meet—became an obsession for him. Turning poetry, and literature entire, into a compass was his objective. As stated in "*Un poeta,*" poetry was an act of redemption for the modern man trapped in an alienating, burdensome universe. In the fifties Paz became a signatory to the tension of the Cold War and, also, in his words, "to the upheaval and changes on the periphery of developing nations." It was a season of intense soul-searching: infuriated by Sartre's flaccid

support of the Soviet regime (it reminded him
of a sentence by Enrique Ramírez y Ramírez:
"The revolution is a sin but a sin that works"),
he made a "public break" in a piece he published
in *Sur,* acknowledging truths about communism
most artists refused to recognize at the time. (In
English, it is included in *On Poets and Others.*)
He also published an essay documenting Stalin's
concentration camps.

Then he underwent a complete ideological
turnaround. The occasion was Fidel Castro's
revolutionary movement in Cuba in 1958–
1959. This was a veritable rite of passage not
only for him but also for an entire generation of
artists in the continent. It sharpened his vision
and made him less patient with earthly utopias.
At first Paz's position, like that of scores of
others including Gabriel García Márquez,
Carlos Fuentes, Julio Cortázar, Mario Vargas
Llosa, and the Spaniard Juan Goytisolo, was one
of unconditional support. In spite of his innate
skepticism, Paz believed in Castro. He trusted
that a more hopeful direction had to be taken to
solve the problems of Hispanic society—
poverty, lack of collective self-respect, and
governmental corruption. And when, in 1966,

the Argentine Ernesto "Ché" Guevara gave up
his high status in the new Havana regime to
continue his struggle on behalf of the peasants
and the working class in Bolivia and elsewhere
in South America, the euphoria was overpower-
ing: a new era had begun. But Paz's applause was
not from the heart. By now he had serious
doubts. He understood that his progressive
disenchantment with ideological utopias was
explosive enough to generate a clash with his
peers. After all, in Latin America literati are seen
as a voice for the oppressed and silenced, a
factor in the resistance against the status quo.
His response could be seen as reactionary and
complacent.

After his break from communism in *Sur,*
he felt liberated but awaited a response. None
came. Silence, it was clear, was the way his peers
chose to react—*el ninguneo.* Clearly his position
infuriated many Marxist believers, and Paz was
accused of treason, but as a heresy and not in
print. When, in the late sixties, Castro finally
confessed his loyalty to Moscow's politburo,
Paz's criticism became even louder and also
more insistent. And in the seventies, attacking
apologists for the Soviet influence in Central

America, he eulogized the dissident Aleksandr Solzhenitsyn as a symbol of antitotalitarianism who "passed the test of history." His political coming of age is also tangible in other occasional pieces, reviews and essays on major historical events and personalities in which he ridiculed left-wingers and portrayed himself as a champion of democracy. The equation of transformation with revolution now seemed to him utterly preposterous.

Probably in response to his disenchantment, Paz traveled to India and Japan. The voyage allowed him to embark on a study of Eastern mysticism and philosophy that intensified while he was, for six years, ambassador to India. His diplomatic duties allowed him to visit Sri Lanka, Afghanistan, Burma, Thailand, Singapore, and Cambodia. This peripatetic model—the intellectual as ceaseless wayfarer—is not unlike those of Orwell, Edmund Wilson, Arthur Koestler, and even Hemingway. To trek is to think in motion, to be Tocqueville again: a "stranger" with a conscience, a smart tourist and partial chronicler of one's age.

Paz also discovered that he was in favor of dialogue, of peaceful change, and against any

form of destructiveness. In his collection entitled *Convergences,* and even before, probably
dating back to the forties; his object of worship
was Charles Fourier, a Frenchman of Bretonian
lineage who celebrated the body and stood as a
challenger to industrialism and consumerism, a
man committed to the twin goals of erotic
freedom and sexual equality. It was the late
sixties and early seventies, and the climate of
rebellion and hippie life put him in touch with
Buddhism and Oriental mysticism. The body,
microcosm of the universe entire, captured his
attention. The language of the body, its "rebellion," became a bewitchment.

In one of his most difficult yet rewarding
works, *Conjunctions and Disjunctions,* a tour de
force of 1969, Paz applied Claude Lévi-Strauss's
categories to distinguish between *cara* and
culo—"face" and "backside"—as metaphorical
oppositions present in Quevedo's poetry and in
the cartoons of José Guadalupe Posada, a
Mexican lampooner famous during the Mexican
Revolution. (By chance, I read the book to-
gether with Kundera's *Unbearable Lightness of
Being,* in which the narrator discusses Jesus
Christ's excrement as divine object.) Ranging

among such topics as Taoism, Goya's pictorial art, the inflammatory essays by Jonathan Swift, and the eschatological poetry of Juan Ramón Jiménez, Paz pursues his objective of understanding the duality in man: heaven and earth, love and hate, the bodily and the spiritual. The book, full of energy, curiosity, and intelligence, is, in Irving Howe's words, the product of "an intellectual one-man band who performs everything from five-finger sonatas to full-scale symphonies and even electronic music"—an extraordinary analysis of the many contradictions that make us human and of how the body is represented in Western pictorial art and letters.

Tlatelolco. The word itself is painful. The volcano of animosity and dissent brought about by the incident it stands for made Paz a cause célèbre in 1968, when he resigned his post as ambassador to India in protest against a shameless act of repression by the Mexican government. The year was marked by student demonstrations in Prague, Berkeley, and Paris. Just as the Olympic Games were about to take place, students in Mexico organized too. Trying to avoid international embarrassment, Mexico's ruling party, the PRI, in power since 1929, foolishly shot itself in the foot. It sent tanks to Tlatelolco Square and a slaughter took place. (Elena Poniatowska produced a memorable chronicle of these events in *Massacre in Mexico*.) Paz understood the challenge of the times: he denounced the regime, and thus became a voice of conscience. Intellectuals worldwide greeted the resignation with enthusiasm.

To me this decision by Paz is admirable. Ours is a most puzzling age. It is often difficult to know what to do, but he was sure that, as Wilson stated, "a conviction that is genuine will always come through—that is, if one's work is sound." With courage and conviction, he distanced himself from the atrocities and their perpetrators, but he refused to be a mere by-stander. He wrote "Posdata," an appendix to *The Labyrinth of Solitude*. (In English it is titled "The Other Mexico" and appears in the Grove edition of 1985 along with an interview and two more essays: "Mexico and the United States" and "The Philanthropic Ogre.") And in the next decades he produced an array of pieces that recorded the nation's search for a more demo-cratic system. In the end, a change did occur, but too late for Paz to see it: in an election in 2000, the PRI lost the presidency to Vicente Fox, a candidate of the conservative PAN.

Paz's character as an intellectual also came into full view in his capacity as editor. I have reflected much on this facet of his career and sought inspiration in it as I launched my own periodical, *Hopscotch: A Cultural Review*. As editor, I constantly try to see the forest *and* the trees. I want the journal to offer a range of opinions and trends and also to be an instrument that might even foster a cultural renaissance of sorts. A balance between literature and commerce is not always easy to achieve, nor is a marriage between what an editor looks for and what he finds. These reflections bring forth in me many thoughts about the history of magazines in the Hispanic world. Literary supplements and journals of opinion have always played a major role in the shaping of culture. They have served as gathering points to catalyze transnational artistic moods, crystallize current political opinions, and promote intellectual trends that would otherwise never reach the largest segment of the population. They also function as ideological galaxies in which secondary voices endlessly rotate around an imperious dictatorial figure, making them temples of adoration and sacrifice in which to pay tribute to a *caudillo* and, simultaneously, from which to orchestrate fanciful battles to debunk an enemy. By the same token, their autocratic editors use them as springboards for their own personal and artistic purposes.

The prestigious Cuban magazine *Orígenes* (active between 1944 and 1956) launched an esthetic renewal promoting seriousness and artistic commitment regardless of political affiliation. Initiated by high-caliber figures such as Virgilio Piñiera and Cintio Vitier, and controlled by José Lezama Lima, the periodical, while mapping out Cuban culture, pretty much behaved as a centralized, undemocratic, self-generating system. Similarly, Ortega y Gasset's long-running *Revista de Occidente,* interested in natural and human sciences, as well as in literature and pictorial art, promoted German philosophy (Oswald Spengler, Max Scheler, Ludwig Klages) in the Iberian peninsula and throughout Latin America from 1923 on. The magazine served Ortega y Gasset as a springboard for his own ideas and made them extremely influential. And *Sur,* founded by Victoria Ocampo, where Borges published his most enduring and dazzling essays and stories, for decades exerted an incredible influence on Argentine culture, welcoming European literary fashions and accusing pro-Soviet and pro-aboriginal writers of obscurantism.

As a result of the insularity and peculiar metabolism of the Hispanic intelligentsia, commanding journals of this stature can flourish only in cosmopolitan centers like Buenos Aires, Havana, Ciudad de México, Madrid, and Barcelona. But their impact reaches far beyond urban and national borders, as is the case of *Vuelta,* a monthly magazine of enormous influence, controlled by a small literary cadre. From its troublesome birth in 1976 until its closure in 1998 immediately after Paz's death, it gravitated around him and no one else. Published in a southern suburb of Ciudad de México and sold in major Spanish-speaking capitals, as well as in select bookstores throughout Europe and the United States, its handsome,

refined pages regularly featured works by an
international cast of contributors from Milan
Kundera and Daniel Bell to Susan Sontag and
Hans Magnus Enzensberger, from Leszek

Kolakowski to George Steiner, from Irving
Howe to Joseph Brodsky, from Derek Walcott to
Charles Tomlinson. But they also included a
vast number of Spanish-speaking counterparts
(Mario Vargas Llosa, Jorge Edwards, Javier
Marías, Guillermo Cabrera Infante, Fernando
Savater, et al.), thus promoting the Bolivarian
view of the hemisphere and the Iberian penin-
sula as a rich mosaic of dreams and ideas.

Paz's primary interests, coloring the journal
from the beginning, were the crossroads I have
alluded to—the juxtapositions of history and
politics and of politics and literature. An average
of eight of the twelve monthly issues contained a
text written by him. The topics: his own life, the
1994 *campesino* uprising in Chiapas, the Berlin
Wall, the pictorial art of Wolfgang Paalen, Sor
Juana Inés de la Cruz's intricate intellectual
universe, Anglo-Saxon poetry, and so on. He
might also publish a new poem or a translation
of a Chinese, French, or English classic. All in
all, Paz's work was invariably lucid and insight-

ful: in full command of a vast array of knowledge, through powerful arguments he allowed readers to see the world anew.*

By then he had learned that deep at heart he was allergic to any form of dogmatism and isolationism, to any systematic practice of intolerance as a form of social control. He championed a view of Hispanic culture as deeply rooted in its pre-Columbian past but fully devoted to inserting itself into the banquet of Western civilization. Not surprisingly, *Vuelta* served to open up Mexican literature to outside forces and to promote Pan-Americanism among the region's intelligentsia. Much like its predecessor *Sur,* its implicit dream always was to become a vehicle for Latin America's collective

* A number of studies on literary magazines in Latin America have appeared recently, but unfortunately none devoted to *Vuelta.* See especially John King, *Sur: A Study of the Argentine Literary Journal and Its Role in the Development of a Culture, 1931–1970* (Cambridge: Cambridge University Press, 1986); and Jesús J. Barquet, *Consagración de La Habana: Las peculiaridades del grupo Orígenes en el proceso cultural cubano* (Miami: Iberian Studies Institute, North-South Center, University of Miami, 1992).

search for democracy and fight against dictator-ship, *un lugar abierto*, an "open place," and a site of intellectual and artistic convocation, as evidence that Hispanics are not part of the so-called Second or Third World but, in Paz's own words, "contemporaries of the rest of human-kind."

But the magazine and its environs were never without major contradictions, and the content of its pages could not but reflect the fractured Mexican literary scene, divided, since the early days of our century, into opposing crowds, each unified by a political stand and dancing around a leading luminary. Indeed, others before Paz functioned as the nation's literary caudillos, including Alfonso Reyes, an essayist and Hellenist scholar once described by Borges as "the greatest prose writer in Spanish in any era."

Nevertheless, in spite of its universalist, antiprovincial stand, *Vuelta* was more receptive than projective. At least a third of the essays and reviews in every issue were translations from European and U.S. contributors. As for its original Latin American material, aside from Paz's own, it was very infrequently translated

and reprinted elsewhere. In an environment
long known for pirating texts from international
periodicals, *Vuelta* was a pioneer in fulfilling its
copyright obligations: it regularly requested
permission to reprint articles from, say, the *New
York Review of Books* or *Nouvelle Revue Française,*
and, unlike its competitors in Mexico and
elsewhere in the Hispanic world, it paid its
monetary dues. But its honesty does not com-
pensate for its dependence on other languages
and cultures. *Vuelta* always took considerably
more than it gave. That is, although Paz's hope
was to bring the Hispanic intelligentsia to
Western civilization, it often seemed the other
way around.

As a living organism, the monthly was in
constant change. It consistently reflected Paz's
rotating political beliefs. In its almost twenty
years of life, it crystallized his anticommunism
and his animosity toward the Mexican government in 1976, his subsequent partnership with
top national politicians of the PRI, and his
concerns with the country's fragile civil and
financial stability at the time. Overall, what
unified its pages was a passive, dilettantish
philosophy: to observe and to contemplate,

reflect, and meditate seemed to be *Vuelta's* uniform attitude, never to act to change the way things were. Its young staff—the average age was thirty-five—was not known for encouraging hard-hitting journalism or debate about national and continental affairs; instead, it often sponsored discursive literary essays about abstract esthetic issues and literary subjects, which assumed a high level of sophistication among readers. Rather than debating the national crisis of confidence in Mexico's untrustworthy politicians and repressive government system, for example, it supported global conferences on transcendental subjects such as "the experience of freedom," inviting international specialists. Throughout its history the journal appears to have been uninvolved in local issues and isolated in a self-created bubble.

The question of authenticity returns. One could argue, of course, that just because *Vuelta's* offices were south of the Rio Grande, the magazine was not obligated to reflect solely on national and Third World issues. After all, the Latin American intelligentsia, like all others, is allowed a dose of dilettantism. Besides, *Vuelta* was not the first journal to turn its back on regional problems: Ortega y Gasset and Victoria Ocampo often endorsed similar platforms in *Revista de Occidente* and *Sur.* Paz's pages no doubt fulfilled an escapist function, vis-à-vis other Mexican monthlies (*Epoca, Proceso, Nexos*) in which hard-hitting journalism was practiced and antigovernment views were often expressed.

Whenever its editorial policy did opt for a more active involvement in local affairs, it came as a result of Mexico undergoing a deep crisis, like the one in 1982 involving the nationalization of the bank industry, or else every six years, as presidential elections were held. When the nation lacked confidence in its politicians, and specifically in reaction to the assassinations of Luis Donaldo Colosio and Ernesto Ruíz Massieu, for example, the magazine reevaluated its principles and took a more decisive, participatory attitude. And during the decisive presidential elections of 1994, in which Ernesto Zedillo Ponce de León was declared winner, it published occasional news analyses and opinion pieces on Mexico's need for democracy. It also included a special supplement, "Chiapas: Days of Challenge," dealing with the Ejército Zapatista de Liberación Nacional. But if previous outbursts of commitment were any sign, this editorial direction was likely to fade away the moment the crisis was resolved.

Paz's old-time coeditor and right hand, Enrique Krauze, was an iconoclastic historian interested in revolutionary heroes and in Mexico's monolithic political structure. While concerned with national and international matters, he was careful enough to have a cordial relationship with Mexico's government. In fact, it was a well-known fact that while the country has undergone an abrupt modernization since the end of World War II, it has also experienced impossible corruption, guerrilla warfare, and urban unrest, and Latin America in general has been torn apart by foreign invasions and military coups. But readers browsing through *Vuelta*'s past issues would learn very little about it. In a region where leftist intellectuals were in the pay of petty tyrants, the journal often discussed diplomatic issues in an obnoxiously abstract philosophical fashion. Krauze's pieces approached long-dead historical personalities like Humboldt, Hernán Cortés, Cuauhtémoc, Porfirio Díaz, Zapata, and Villa with a critical eye, but his comments on contemporary government matters, unless a crisis made them urgent and unavoidable, were comparatively shy and without edge. Rather than inviting opposing parties to discuss their differences, the magazine frequently preached to believers. Its foundation was predictable, and so was its message. (It was Krauze who closed *Vuelta* permanently in 1998 and quickly launched his own literary monthly: *Letras Libres*.)

On the other hand, in retrospect *Vuelta* ought to be commended for its independent spirit—and here again, its pages mirror the contradictions of its environment. Because the paper industry is government run, and because a considerable segment of the advertisements in every Mexican periodical comes from state institutions, freedom and integrity of opinion are often at stake. With a circulation of 15,000, *Vuelta* depended on national and international subscriptions as well as on publicity, but only some 30 percent of its ads came from the government. Nevertheless, private corporations such as Televisa, the largest television consortium in the southern hemisphere, with close ties to the ruling party, were strong advertising supporters, and in the eyes of the average

Mexico reader, that amounted to being hand-cuffed. In the past, whenever periodicals have proven too critical of the state, the government has threatened to interrupt their ads and boycott paper supplies. But in spite of its condescending politics and as a result of its financial autonomy (achieved mainly through private advertising), *Vuelta* was never involved in a head-on confrontation with the authorities. That is, aside from it very conception. Its birth was the result of a brutal government takeover.

Paz had more than his share of experience dealing with literary magazines. In his adolescence, between 1931 and 1943, he had edited the exciting and short-lived *Barandal, Cuadernos del Valle de México,* and *El Hijo Pródigo,* through which he had introduced dozens of foreign voices to Mexican audiences and where he had forged his essayistic style. Later, after a brief incubating period, he helped to make *Plural,* a periodical published as a supplement by the newspaper *Excélsior,* into an exquisite literary journal. It had high editorial standards, and its contributors did indeed inject a refreshing new life into Mexican letters. Paz quickly invited a number of major figures to write for *Plural* and promoted Mexico as a meeting place for discussing critical thought and inspiring good writing.

As time went by, however, *Excélsior* as a whole came to be recognized as a focus of antigovernment feeling. Moreover, its views often clashed with Paz's. Expectedly, in July 1976, Mexico's President Luis Echeverría Alvarez, angry with its staff and having exhausted other venues to quiet the criticism targeted at him at home and abroad, ordered the army to intervene. The newspaper's offices were taken over, its employees dismissed. The scandal turned out to have positive consequences. While both the newspaper and *Plural* continued under new stewardship, Julio Scherer García and Paz, each supported by private funds, launched separate monthly magazines: *Proceso,* edited by the former, was devoted to "accurate, honest journalism that [was] ready to denounce corruption wherever it might be found"; Paz, in turn, orchestrated a reorganization of his editorial staff and began *Vuelta*. He was sixty-two—a totem, a T. S. Eliot–like figure in Hispanic American letters. Anything he touched he quickly turned into gold.

Eventually, like *Les Temps Moderns* in its

relation to Sartre, *Vuelta*, even more than *Plural*, came to be known as Paz's instrument of cultural control—his extremity, a permanent source of congratulation, a compass signaling the many influences of his fascinating mind. From its first issue its editorial principles were clear: to leave behind any form of provincialism, to reflect on international events from a philosophical perspective. In its first issue, Paz argued that *Vuelta* was not a beginning but, as its title implies, "a return." In 1981, in a commemorative essay on its fifth anniversary, he described the magazine as born out of a desire to oppose state power and Marxism as an ideological doctrine. He reinstated the magazine's utopian objective to create a platform where one could simultaneously find the writer's imagination and modern critical thinking.

But Paz's democratic wishes could not fight against the well-known, essentially dictatorial facet of his personality. Consequently, the magazine never included a correspondence section where ideas could be freely exchanged, and left-wing writers such as García Márquez, Cortázar, José Agustín, and Paco Ignacio Taibo II, although their books might be reviewed, were generally excluded from its content. Paradoxically, dogmatism was not only attacked but also practiced in its pages: views differing from Paz's and the staff's were pushed aside and ridiculed, never debated. As a result, readers interested in the whole spectrum of contemporary trends in Latin American thought and literature hardly received a comprehensive, uncensored view. *Vuelta* routinely ignored Hispanic pulp fiction, and either looked down on or handled with unusual care the work of regional celebrities with whom Paz was at odds, personally and politically—particularly his nemesis, Fuentes.

To read its pages was to suppose that most people in Mexico, and for that matter in the whole southern hemisphere, were comfortably tolerant of diverse views, not much concerned with local politics, highly literate, and metaphysically driven, which was and is far from true in a nation where 75 percent of the population lives in poverty and 49 percent is still illiterate. This helps explains why, as a counterpoint to *Vuelta,* left-wing Mexican intellectuals launched *Nexos,* a monthly edited by the well-known journalist Miguel Aguilar Camín, skeptical of abstract cosmopolitanism, devoted to *Realpolitik* and trendy literary movements. The Mexican intelligentsia, unlike that of Argentina or Cuba, is polarized, zealously moving between these two major periodicals, which often waste their energy discrediting the enemy.

To understand why throughout Latin America *Vuelta* was largely considered a conservative publication, one needs to follow Paz's own ideological journey from the Spanish Civil War to the fall of the Berlin Wall. At first a fervent supporter of Socialism and an enthusiast of Castro's Cuban Revolution, he grew disappointed in the late sixties with naive utopian thought and turned against the Havana regime when he learned of its alignment with the Soviet Union. At a time when the Latin American left was still stuck in its dogmatic Stalinism, he denounced the Gulag, supported Aleksandr Solzhenitsyn, and in the pages of *Plural* was in favor of democratic change, not abrupt revolutions. His intellectual development, and that of *Vuelta,* pushed him more to the center: he declared himself in favor of an open market of ideas in the Hispanic world and, while still viewing dictatorship as the region's major evil, he grew more complacent about the ruling party. His seventieth birthday, in 1984, and then again his eightieth were jointly celebrated with great fanfare by the ruling party and Televisa, with TV programs, conferences, and museum exhibits. Paz was seen by a large segment of Mexico's population as disconnected from the nation's new artistic, antiestablishment trends, as a close friend of the status quo, and as an ally of the United States, his magazine as a reactionary organ of Mexico's intellectual right. Anybody critical of Paz as a caudillo was either excluded from or viciously attacked in *Vuelta,* as was the case with José Emilio Pacheco, an internationally renowned poet targeted as an enemy by some of Paz's supporters. And yet, when Pacheco's house in Ciudad de México was involved in a shootout, Paz's journal quickly published a manifesto denouncing violence in all forms.

Although each issue, when compared to similar periodicals in the United States, sold a small number of copies, its impact on Latin American intellectual life cannot be overestimated. Young writers dreamed of having manuscripts accepted and their books reviewed in it. By the late eighties its owners opened an ultimately ill-fated branch in Buenos Aires, called *Vuelta Sudamericana,* and it also expanded to the book business, launching, in 1987, Editorial *Vuelta,* a publishing house largely devoted to translations and to promoting the works of its contributors. These efforts were crowned in 1993, when Paz and his staff were awarded Spain's Prince of Asturias Prize for their major contribution to the development of Hispanic culture. It was a known secret, though, that Paz, already in his eighties and often found at home alone writing or abroad lecturing, only occasionally went to the offices of *Vuelta.* Whatever business he conducted, he did mainly by phone. And yet his shadow cast a heavy pall upon the magazine's future. Indeed, its demise is probably explainable by the sheer size of that shadow.

To be honest, dilettantism in Latin America has always had a healthy life, particularly since the late nineteenth century when the so-called *modernistas,* led by Martí and Darío, championed a literature obsessed with French symbolism and Parnassianism. Paz's magazine was an embodiment of the Hispanic intellectual contradiction between commitment and withdrawal: it supported an image of the intellectual as a creature devoted to producing high-quality writing, concerned with world affairs, but too individualistic to participate in making history. Issue after issue, *Vuelta* was a pleasure to read: carefully edited, and almost all of its contributors, native Spanish writers and otherwise, consummate stylists and literary devotees. But it served also as a temple of adoration with Paz on its supreme altar, and as a compass to his intricate, extraordinary mind.

In *Itinerary,* Paz reviewed his life from 1929 to 1993. He concluded:

> I realize that [my] pilgrimage has brought me back to my beginning. Faced with the contemporary panorama I feel that same dissatisfaction I experienced when young confronting the modern world. I think, as I used to, that we should change it, although I no longer have the strength or youth to attempt it. Nor do I know how to go about it. Nobody does. The ancient methods were not only inefficient but foul.

Does this disillusioned conclusion write off my experience and that of my generation? No: the geometric figure that symbolizes it is the spiral, a line that continuously returns to its starting point and that continuously distances itself more and more from it. The spiral never returns. We never return to the past and thus every return is a beginning. The questions I asked myself at the start are the same ones I ask myself now . . . and they are different.

I find the image of the spiral appealing: it is a *continuum*, a curve traced by a point that moves around and around in the same plane and that simultaneously ascends or descends, depending on how one looks at it. Paz also went inward and outward. Some three decades after the publication of *The Labyrinth of Solitude*, he produced another masterpiece, his second. Cyril Connolly once said that "the more books we read, the sooner we perceive that the only function of a writer is to produce a masterpiece. No other task is of any consequence." Paz was allowed a couple and that is a prize onto itself. At the age of sixty-eight, he published *Sor Juana,*

or, the Traps of Faith, an outstanding nonstand-
ard biography of the Mixcoac-born nun. Released in 1982, it was a mystifying game of
mirrors: a contemporary poet looking into the
past to explain his own intellectual journey.
Mixing historical research, anthropological
insights, personal speculation, and autobiographical allusions, the thick volume analyzes
Sor Juana Inés de La Cruz's sophisticated style
through a wide range of topics like church
activities, Neoplatonism, courtly love, medieval
Spanish poetry, and the political and social
foundation of the Americas.

Paz's earliest education occurred in
Mixcoac, a southern suburb of the nation's
capital, which during colonial times included
the Carmelite convent where Sor Juana Inés de
La Cruz, one of Paz's idols, lived from youth
until her early death in 1695. Sor Juana was a
protofeminist nun and Latin American's foremost pre-Independence intellectual, who wrote
the celebrated poem *First Dream.* (I have written
a lengthy essay on her that is part of the anthology *Poems, Protest, and a Dream,* translated by
Margaret Sayers Peden.) This geographical link
between Paz and Sor Juana nurtured his view of

Mexican history as a pyramid: each person, each epoch, he believed, established its own identity by finding its place on top of proceeding generations. The present, then, is a sum of pasts eternally recycled, and every contemporary citizen a continuation, a reincarnation of those alive before. And so Sor Juana lives *in* and *through* Paz.

The most engaging segment of *Sor Juana* is devoted to the poem *First Dream,* drafted in 1692, in which the protagonist is the human mind traveling in a night's journey through heaven and earth to decipher the terrestrial and spiritual enigmas of life. For a long time this puzzling text has left a rich trail of contradictory interpretations. Paz's own interpretation centers on Sor Juana's religiosity and her implicit conflict of interests: as a Catholic living in a Carmelite convent, the Mexican nun could neither question God's role in the creation of the universe nor attempt to clarify those doubts left to faith. At the same time, her intelligence could not consent to reducing the human mind to a timid, paralyzed entity without the courage to question its surroundings.

Much like the explanation of Maimonides's

Guide for the Perplexed offered by Leo Strauss, an influential conservative professor at the University of Chicago and Allan Bloom's mentor, Paz's argument holds that the nun placed a number of crucial clues throughout the text to enable astute readers to discover her hidden intention. From his perspective, the poem is not only a nightlong journey into religious certainty; it is also a defense of poetry. This interpretation also applies to Sor Juana's "Response to Sor Filotea de La Cruz," a letter the nun wrote in 1691 after her confessor accused her of being too bold a woman, a threat to the male-oriented milieu. After careful reflection, she renounced her personal library and literary career. Paz shows how, as society first protected then attacked her talents, her final action held a double meaning: it is simultaneously a renunciation and a triumph of the literary will, a sign of her knowledge that posterity is her only true judge.

Perhaps because of a longstanding resistance to the public confessional mode, to the communication of inner fears, the literary genre of autobiography is not well regarded in the Hispanic world. That is why the urgent message in Paz's book is such a refreshing treat and an example of what cultural criticism ought to be: finding the particular in the universal, it unravels the enigma of a people's collective psyche by explaining a person's existential plight. (I dream one day of embarking on a similar quest: an examination of the clash between politics and literature in the twentieth century through the magisterial figure of Gabriel García Márquez— not a biography per se, but a summa that should serve as a living mural, at once panoramic and deep.) One can hardly ask anything more of a book.

Before the publication of Paz's book, Sor Juana was but a shadow, an academic delicacy— today she is a key to the collective identity. Paz's political motivation for such an enterprise is once again clear: anxious to be fully technologized, contemporary Mexico runs the risk of losing itself in the labyrinth of modernity. The solution is to look into the mirror of the past, to be loyal to the nation's foundation. Sor Juana's struggle to make faith and intellect compatible, to be recognized as a half-native and half-Iberian hybrid and respected as a woman in a dogmatic male-dominated universe, is not unlike Paz's desire to retain the poet's power to

understand and decipher a world easily cor-
rupted by consumerism and idolatry, his hope to
perpetuate highbrow culture, and his dream to
be a Europeanized Mexican.

The style and content of *The Traps of Faith,*
and Paz's other essays of the time, are indebted
to his passion for structuralism, a school of
thought with which he identified in the 1960s
because of its interest in "primitive" modes of
thought. His intellectual curiosity led him to
write a booklet on Lévi-Strauss and, as well, to
attempt, with little success, an explanation of his
own poetry in structural categories. After that,
he became enchanted with a handful of other
stars in the French constellation: George
Bataille, the Marquis de Sade ("after whom no
one has dared to discover an atheist society"),
and other Parisian writers interested in exploring
sexuality and intrigued by bodily signs and
metaphors.

Among my personal favorite books by Paz
is *The Double Flame,* a meditation on the
whirlpool of love and ardor, topics that might
seem untimely in 1993 for a man born at the
outbreak of World War I. But the book is a
product of immense wisdom, and wisdom is

67
:::

accumulative, though not knowledge. Here Paz
is patient in his observations and encyclopedic
in scope. He allows himself sociological, anthropological, historical, and literary explorations,
but, as in *The Labyrinth of Solitude,* does so
through an "I" that is nonscientific. The journey
includes no statistics, no historical back up, no
academic qualifiers. He simply does what he
always did best: he uses his poetic voice to
engage us in a rendezvous of ideas, all of which
makes the volume a synthesis of sorts.

Sex, he claims, places humans in the
animal kingdom and has reproduction as its
goal; eroticism, on the other hand, is a socialized
form of sexuality transfigured by our dreams;
and love is altogether more abstract, at once an
amatory sentiment and a concept developed
during a certain historical period. He rightly
argues that, beginning with Freud, too many
scholars have devoted themselves to the study of
sexuality, while feelings such as love and friendship, less visible, more evasive, remain largely
unexplored.

Paz delves into the varieties of love
throughout the ages, from courtly to marital
love, from the mystic's love of God to the

nineteenth-century concept of patriotism as love for one's nation. And be devotes the last segment of *The Double Flame* to recent studies of the mind that, in his eyes, say very little about who we are and why we feel attracted to each other.

His ultimate thesis is that our society is plagued by erotic permissiveness, placing the stability and continuity of love in jeopardy, and that the difficult encounter between two humans attracted to each other has lost importance, a development that he believes threatens our psychological and cultural foundations. He navigates with enviable ease through intellectual history, pondering Buddhism, Taoism, Gnosticism, and the Bible, Greek and Hellenistic thinkers, and medieval, renaissance, and modern artists. In one page he might be commenting on Santa Teresa de Jesús, and in the next discussing Mumsaid Shikubu, Ramón López Velarde, and John Donne. The work's structure is deliberately capricious, allowing Paz to explore a theme for the sheer pleasure of it. That, I think, is his greatest asset. This seems to be the way his mind functioned: he first chose a topic and then let the train of thought loose, totally free—to invoke a maxim of surrealism. Author and reader are never bored; in fact, they are constantly surprised.

By this time, Paz had become a dictator. His voice was authoritative but also authoritarian. Once, in an essay, I defined him as a tyrant. A storm of attacks descended on me. But the image is not far-fetched. A tyrant, in the words of Norman Manea, is a despotic knight of utopia. "Everything has to do with him—and his favorite world is everything. . . . The rest is ridiculous." Indeed, Paz's ultimate transformation as a man of politics is embodied in the conservative ideology he supported in his maturity: from rebel to consenter. From the seventies to the nineties, he slowly became a trenchant anticommunist and a visible supporter of Mexico's oligarchy and status quo. His imposing figure as a literary lion—between 1977 and 1990 he was awarded the Jerusalem Prize, the Premio Ollín Yoliztli, the Cervantes Prize, the Neustadt Prize, and the Nobel Prize, among others—made him intransigent. He was a demigod: the orchestrator of history. This transformation is troublesome but also inevitable. Paz himself explained it in the quote from

Itinerary: "I think, as I used to, that we should change it, although I no longer have the strength or youth to attempt it. Nor do I know how to go about it." A factor in this omnipresence was his productivity: the frequency with which he wrote essays and books, while traveling around the globe, was simply stunning.

A facet of his career I personally admire, one nurtured in these last stages too, was translation. As I have suggested, Paz translated gems of foreign cultures into his own language. It was an act of appropriation, as all translations are, and Paz exercised a will to power unconfined by cultural and linguistic boundaries. By representing important works of other literatures, he annexed and interjected everything non-Mexican. His efforts produced personal versions of poems by Charles Tomlinson, Elizabeth Bishop (her work during her Brazilian period), and the Swede Artur Lundkvist, as well as a number of Chinese and Japanese poets (including Li Po, Wang Wei, and Su Shih, Kakinomoto Hitomaro, Matsuo Basho, and Kobayashi Issa). Paz also translated verses by Fernando Pessoa, Mallarmé, Apollinaire, Gerard de Nerval, John Donne, e.e. cummings, William

Carlos Williams, and Ezra Pound, and more often than not prefaced his renditions with brilliant mini-essays. (His best translations into Spanish were included in *Versiones y diversiones;* his views on the art of translation are part of *Confrontaciones,* known also as *El signo y el garabato.*) These exercises distilled a unique structure: with the help of appendixes and personal commentary at the end of the text, Paz shows how wise and incomparable he really is.

Indeed, looking back at his career as a translator, I feel the need to highlight at this point an earlier endeavor that merits a paragraph: a curious anthology, at least in the eyes of English-speaking and French readers, entitled *Mexican Poetry.* Compiled in 1958 under the sponsorship of UNESCO and originally published by Indiana University Press, the book dates to a time when Paz was immersing himself as a researcher in the nation's colonial and independent periods. It includes verses by Bernardo to Balbuena, Ramón López Velarde, and other national poets—all serviceably if somewhat quirkily translated by Samuel Beckett. (As far as I know, this is Beckett's only translation from the Spanish.) For Paz, the anthology provided an opportunity to set forth his aesthetic views of how literature developed within Mexican borders. Indeed, the anthology, which is accompanied in the American edition by a preface by the Oxford classics scholar C. M. Bowra, and in French by an essay by Paul Claudel, features Paz as the ultimate interpreter of Mexican culture, the door to its secret codes and bizarre manifestations. He ponders the impact of the Iberian poets Quevedo, Lope de Vega, and Góngora in colonial letters; studies the impact of Latin America's modernist movement on late nineteenth- and early twentieth-century versifiers like Rubén Darío, Amado Nervo, Enrique González Martínez, and José Juan Tablada; and reaches across the Pacific and Atlantic to link Mexican letters to Japanese, Arabic, European, and Hindu art. In a spectacular display of knowledge and lucidity, he finds a way to make the poetry in his native country a showcase of the best and worst in world literature, which is a daunting task indeed. Again the objective here is to turn the universal into a particular or vice versa, all with the effect of showing how Paz is the embodiment of absolute truth.

But even if Paz's intellectual reach seemed inexhaustible, his pen universal, there are lacunae. For reasons I have tackled elsewhere, he refused to address Jewish topics altogether. Also, he never produced an essay on Latin America's literary boom of the 1960s. In a connoisseur constantly redrafting history, this particular absence is intriguing, especially when one thinks how the works of García Márquez and his colleagues have been compared to the renewal of Russian letters in the second half of the nine-teenth century, in the writings of Tolstoy, Dostoyevski, Chekhov, and Turgenev. Occasion-ally, Paz did release an obituary, as when Cortázar died in 1984 (although, not surpris-ingly, he devoted most of the space to recollect-ing his Paris years and only in passing men-tioned the Argentine's life and work).

This silence, however, is just on paper. In real life, Paz had a long list of well-publicized quarrels with Fuentes, Vargas Llosa, and other writers from the region with whom friendship was always a difficult affair. Take the Peruvian, whose intellectual pilgrimage, similar to Paz's, witnessed a swing from active support of the Cuban Revolution to a Reaganite promotion of

a free-market pluralistic approach to Latin
America. Invited to a conference called "The
Experience of Freedom," organized by *Vuelta* in
1989, Vargas Llosa took the opportunity to
portray Mexico as a perfect dictatorship, thus
embarrassing President Carlos Salinas de Gortari
who traveled the world selling his country as a
democracy and hated to be compared to
Augusto Pinochet or Juan Domingo Perón.
After his remarks, the Peruvian was forced to
leave the country immediately while Paz apolo-
gized. For months Paz stopped speaking to
Vargas Llosa and ceased publishing him in his
magazine. But an armistice was reached. Love,
hate, love, hate. . . .

His friendship with Carlos Fuentes was
marked by the same ambivalence and volatility.
For instance, in an essay written in New Delhi
in 1967, Paz hailed Fuentes as an extraordinary
prose writer, singling out such books as *Los días
enmascarados, Where the Air is Clear, The Death
of Artemio Cruz,* and *Aura.* He celebrated
Fuentes again in 1972. But things went sour,
and they became permanent enemies when, in
the 1980s, Enrique Krauze, with Paz's blessing,
published a negative review in the *New Republic*

of Fuentes's *Myself with Others, Old Gringo,* and other titles. (The piece was reprinted in *Vuelta.*)

Emmanuel Carballo, García Márquez, and other Hispanic intellectuals have also been involved in similarly volatile relationships. I have been a participant in heated intellectual debates (with Eliot Weinberger, among others): they are not present, although they fortify the spirit. Paz was involved in a number of them. I remember one debate with John Barth on postmodernity in the weekly *La jornada semanal;* actually it was more a monologue than a debate, for Barth, if memory serves me well, never answered Paz's accusations. Also, Carballo accused Paz of plagiarism in *The Labyrinth of Solitude,* and García Márquez attacked Paz's complacency, to which Paz responded by describing the author of *Love in the Time of Cholera* as servile to Castro's communism. These clashes often rotated around the role of the intellectual in impoverished nations. In 1977, the Mexican newspaper *El Universal,* for instance, described Paz's poetry as "insufficiently committed to change." It is an ancient harangue: in the early twentieth century the Uruguayan critic José Enrique Rodó similarly accused Rubén Darío of "dandyism." Borges, too, was often portrayed as "an escapist." The accusations are preposterous, of course: an artist's only duty is toward his inner self.

I want to summon one of Camus's famous
dictums, pertinent to these pages: "All revolutionaries end as either oppressors or heretics." From antagonism to consent, Paz the dictator was increasingly portrayed by some as a sellout, one with suspicious ties to the oligarchy—the government's marionette. In 1990, as the announcement of the Nobel Prize awarded to him spread nationwide, Mexico's newspaper headlines were divided; many applauded the prize, but a handful claimed the honor was a gift from President Salinas and also from the immensely powerful Emilio Azcárraga, the owner of Televisa, loyal to the PRI. "God is dead," an interviewee scornfully uttered to a TV camera. Suspicions were fortified by the fact that the award coincided with the multimillion-dollar exhibit *Mexico: Splendors of Thirty Centuries* at the Metropolitan Museum of Art in New York, sponsored by the Mexican president and a close group of rich businessmen. Since Paz happened to be in Manhattan when he received the phone

call from Stockholm, some conjectured about an illicit monetary deal timed with the Nobel selection by the Swedish Academy.

Paz's close association with the centers of power had an inhibiting effect on the literati. In essence, the viewpoint was that his critical "I" no longer could be taken seriously: it was seen as a tentacle of the state, its owner a conformist who traded his dreams for institutional recognition. In *The Devil's Dictionary,* Ambrose Bierce defined a dictator as the head of a nation that prefers the pestilence of despotism to the plague of anarchy. Paz's standing as Mexico's foremost intellectual was in jeopardy: he was a *poète manqué,* no longer a valiant Ulysses. For doesn't the intellectual need autonomy to function? In 1984, on his seventieth birthday, Televisa devoted a series of programs to his work. From that moment on his face appeared regularly on state and private television, and diplomats and academics sought his advice and favor. His home was a required stop for overseas celebrities visiting the country. Yet, in becoming the government's favorite denizen, he also, in the eyes of many, lost his freedom. *El compromiso de la libertad:* many Mexicans, myself included, saw him as handcuffed. Isn't an intellectual by definition antiestablishmentarian? In his late seventies, Paz had transformed himself into an unprogressive patriarch.

But aren't we all blinded by the urgencies of the day? Isn't the road he followed, from rebellion to consent, a road much traveled? This is not an excuse, though: old age is by definition recalcitrant, impatient, uneasy with the rhythms of life, but not everyone betrays the muses of youth. Surely there is much to criticize in Paz: his mammoth ambitions eclipsed others without his ever experiencing misgivings; and though he was a loyal friend, to those beyond his immediate entourage he was abrasive and despotic. The miseries of old age only accentuated these traits.

When he died, he was described as "the *last* intellectual." Was he? The answer is a resounding no. Coincidentally, he died just a few weeks before Alfred Kazin, the Jewish American literary critic responsible for the classic *On Native Ground*. One year younger, Kazin, also original in his voice and another author majestic in the intellectual scope of his oeuvre (though his is less panoramic and pathfinding than the Mexican's), was described in obituaries, especially in the *New York Times,* as "a true intellectual of an almost extinct species." And yet, what does it mean to be the last? Has society changed so much that intellectuals no longer have a role? No doubt Paz's death is a symbol of the end of an era in which the man of letters mattered: ideas were not weightless, and their presence was impossible to ignore. He seized his day: Paz was only possible in the twentieth century—he *and* his time were in unison.

But as we begin the next millennium, intellectuals are still crucial, either as manufacturers of consent, as Chomsky put it, or, through their own internal rhythm, as moral compasses and as fountains of enlightenment. The guru is a fixture in primitive tribes, and his position is also important for us: he verbalizes the unverbalized and reveals undisclosed horizons. Today, as ever, intellectuals must find their niche, just as Paz did. To survive, this endangered species must reinvent itself from A to Z. Words have been replaced by images, and opinions are frighteningly volatile. We all may be less provincial today than a century ago, but truth and certitude are casualties in the age of the "information superhighway." Nothing is sacred anymore; everything is relative. Nowadays, to build bridges across the chambers of the mind, across cultures, one needs not only to write but also to perform, for the only real bombing-planes are on the Internet.

Paz died in Ciudad de México, his home and headquarters, where his telescope looked outward while his microscope looked inward. The metropolis is the scenario of his best poetry. During his lifetime Ciudad de México underwent tremendous change: from a semibucolic locale it grew into an uncontrollable mammoth in which twenty-eight million people were besieged by traffic jams and pollution. While environmental decline seldom occupied him, Paz's effort to turn Ciudad de México into a multifaceted center of enlightenment and civilization is startling. His influence was the kind exercised not by a civic administrator but by an effulgent fashion model. With his magazines *Plural* and *Vuelta,* his dilettantism, his incessant political commentaries, and his love of museums, he made the city far more livable. Without him, it somehow feels—momentarily, at least—bereft of hope. Scores of other intellectuals and artists make their home in Ciudad de

México, but Paz was its brain, its centripetal force, what William H. Gass called "the heart of the heart of the country." In a poem entitled "I Speak of the City," Paz states: "I speak of the city, shepherd of the centuries, mother that gives birth to us and devours us, that creates us and forgets."

The shadow Paz cast over Mexico's intelligentsia was overwhelming for a time. I for one confess to having often thought, in the late nineties, during his last years, how liberating a world without him could be. I had emulated his teachings, but I had come to think of him as a "philanthropic ogre"—the very expression he had used to describe Mexico's government in the sixties, a benign yet suffocating presence, a know-it-all and do-it-all. Envy probably played a part in my attitude toward him, but so did the need to go beyond him, to experience a universe without Big Brother. But the moment he died, the world felt suddenly empty to me: empty of a voice whose echoes I reckon with day and night. Will I too be perceived this way when death transports me to oblivion? Might I be able to produce even a reflection of the fountain of light that Paz generated in my direction? I emulate

him vigorously. Even when I don't write about
him, he looks over my shoulder.

What I admire the most in his quest is its
honesty and its desire to mature. What else
should a writer's career strive for if not maturity?
But maturity is a most elusive stage. When and
how do we reach it in full? We never do, really.
Our only obligation is to produce the best every
day, to live in a marriage—even if it must be a
tumultuous one—with our time. Paz for me is a
paragon of conscience. "That each should in his
house abide," announced Emerson, "Therefore
was the world so wide." Paz's route was his own,
not mine, but behind that route a path is
traceable, and in that path I recognize an
invaluable lesson: society and solitude—how to
make these two compatible? His answer was to
live life in full, alone and with others. To make
oneself present by tracing one's past and betting
on the future.

So many visionaries have their paths cut
short by the accidents of nature. Paz was lucky
to live so long. And he lived with death as his
obsession: individual death, spiritual death,
cosmic death—the death of the mind's eye and
the soul's "I." In life, the invocation of death was

liberating to him, and he experienced that
liberation with passion, for passion is our best
weapon in the battle against nothingness, even
though nothingness in the end prevails.

Montaigne said wisely: "We do not know where
death awaits us, so let us wait for it everywhere.
To practice death is to practice freedom."

An earlier, shorter version of this work appeared in *Transition*. It was reproduced, with slight emendations, in *Art and Anger: Essays on Politics and the Imagination* (University of New Mexico Press, 1996). Thanks are due to Henry Louis Gates, Jr., Kwane Anthony Appiah, and Henry Finder for the assignment and editorial work. Further material was published in *The Nation, Salmagundi,* the *Washington Post,* and *Hopscotch.*

About the Author

Ilan Stavans is Lewis-Sebring Professor of Latin American and Latino Culture at Amherst College. His books include *The Hispanic Condition* (1995), *Art and Anger* (1996), *The Riddle of Cantinflas* (1998), *Mutual Impressions* (1999), and *On Borrowed Words: A Memoir of Language* (2001). Routledge released an anthology of his work under the title *The Essential Ilan Stavans* (2000). He has been a National Book Critics Circle Award nominee and the recipient of the Latino Literature Prize and a Guggenheim Fellowship, among other honors. He has been translated into half a dozen languages.